Fun with Ballet

by

Mae Blacker Freeman

Random House, New York

Contents

ACKNOWLEDGMENTS

The photographs are by the author, and her daughter Marcy, ten years old, posed for them.

Arlene Garver of the Ballet Arts school in Carnegie Hall, New York City, kindly checked all material in this book for technical accuracy.

There exists some latitude in the interpretation of classical ballet, according to the "school" of training and the practices of individual teachers. This book shows methods most generally used in the training of ballet beginners. Based on this, the student will be able to adapt to any variations in her later training.

Introduction

Ballerina is a magic word. Any girl who hears it pictures in her mind a beautiful dancer in a sparkling costume, skimming along on the tips of her toes, seeming to fly like a bird. Of course, the dancer in the girl's imagination usually turns out to be herself!

To dream of being a ballerina is part of a girl's world—the lovely costumes, the satin slippers, the grace and beauty of the movements—everything that appeals to the heart of a young girl.

The exciting part of it all is that every girl can really learn to do ballet dancing. Of course, to become a ballerina requires years of long, hard work. What seems to be effortless dancing is the result of strict training, together with natural gracefulness and a healthy body. But, if she is seriously interested, any girl can become a fairly good dancer, and go even further if her talent and ambition carry through.

In ballet dancing, things must be done in a certain order. Muscles must be trained and strengthened in order to do work never before asked of them. The serious student of dancing will learn the foundations of ballet before going on to the more dramatic and complicated steps, just as a baby must learn to stand before it can walk, and to walk before it can run.

With the help of this book you can learn the first exercises in ballet dancing. And you will discover that the most famous ballerinas limber up every day with exactly these routines.

—MAE BLACKER FREEMAN

As You Begin

Get a pair of soft ballet shoes. You can practice in stocking feet at first, but you will do your best work in regulation ballet shoes and you should get them as soon as you can. They should fit snugly.

Wear a short, close-fitted garment like a bathing suit or a sun suit. The lines of your body and legs must show, so that incorrect positions will not be hidden. For the same reason, tie your hair neatly back off your neck and shoulders. In the photographs, a *leotard* is being worn. This is an inexpensive, knitted costume which dancers wear during practice.

Set aside time every day for regular practice, which is as necessary in ballet dancing as in other arts.

It is good to work facing a large mirror. Even better is to have your mother or some other person work with you. She can watch you practice and help in many ways by counting aloud for you and by checking the pictures and telling you when you are making a mistake that you could not see yourself.

Choose a place to practice where you will have ample room. In a dancing studio there is a hand-rail along the wall. This is called a *barre* and its only purpose is to help keep the balance — it must never be used for support. At home, use a heavy piece of furniture for your *barre*. The footboard of a bed, the back of a heavy chair, or even the edge of the kitchen sink — all of these are good *barres* for work at home. Do not work on a floor that has been waxed — you may slip and be injured.

6

Never look down at your feet when practicing. This throws your whole body out of line and disturbs the balance of your position. That is why you need either a mirror or someone to help you correct errors. 🩰

All of the exercises in this book must be done both RIGHT and LEFT. When instructions show movement with the right leg, you must then turn around and do exactly the same with the left leg. Otherwise you may become a "one-sided" dancer. 🩰 🩰 🩰

Don't hurt your body by forcing; use only gentle firmness and soon you will find that the exercises gradually become easier with daily practice.

All movements must be learned well because later they become parts of complicated dances. Gradual and thorough training will give you smoother, stronger muscles, and a firm basis for going on to become a ballet dancer. 🩰 🩰

The language for ballet is French, just as the language for music is Italian and for sports English. The French words are printed in *italics* and they are listed at the back of the book, with pronunciation, for your reference. Repeat the French name of each exercise as you do it. 🩰

Toe-dancing is called dancing *sur les pointes*. It is quite natural for girls eager to become dancers to want to get up on their toes from the very beginning. Do not be tempted to do this because dancing *sur les pointes* can be done safely and easily only when you are ready for it. The only one who can tell you when you are ready is an experienced dancing teacher. 🩰 🩰 🩰

The Five Positions

Dancing asks your body to use itself differently than usual. For walking, your feet are pointed forward but it has been found that for dancing, the feet and legs must turn outward. Through long experience, the five positions shown in these pictures were found to be the best from which to start all dance steps. As you continue your study of dancing, these positions will become as familiar to you as the notes of music with which you learn songs.

In the following pages of this book you will learn how to train your feet, your legs, your arms—your whole body—to do these positions correctly.

First Position

Stand beside the chair—or whatever you have chosen to be your *barre* —as shown in the picture. Place your left hand on the *barre*. Raise your right arm to the side in a soft curve. Turn your toes outward as far as you comfortably can, keeping your heels touching. Try to turn your leg out all the way from your hip, instead of just pointing the foot outward. This is known as "turn-out" and the better a dancer's turn-out, the better she will dance.

Push your shoulders down. Keep your body straight, directly over your feet. Don't bend your knees even the slightest bit. Tighten your stomach muscles.

Your legs are now in first position.

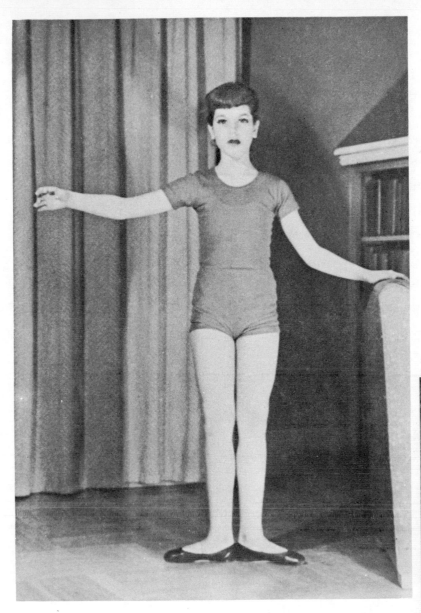

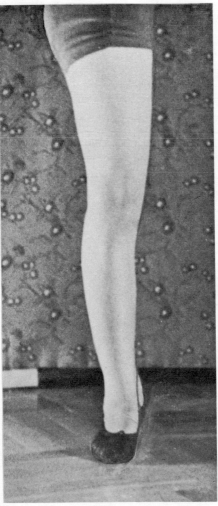

Second Position

Stand in first position. Now slide your right foot to the side for a distance of about the length of your foot.

Keep your weight evenly on both feet, which should be in a straight line under your body. At first you may not be able to turn your feet outward enough, but as your turn-out develops, your hips will become more limber and your feet and legs will turn out more easily.

Don't let your arches roll inward. You can be sure of this by seeing that your little toes do not come off the floor.

Check all the other points mentioned for first position.

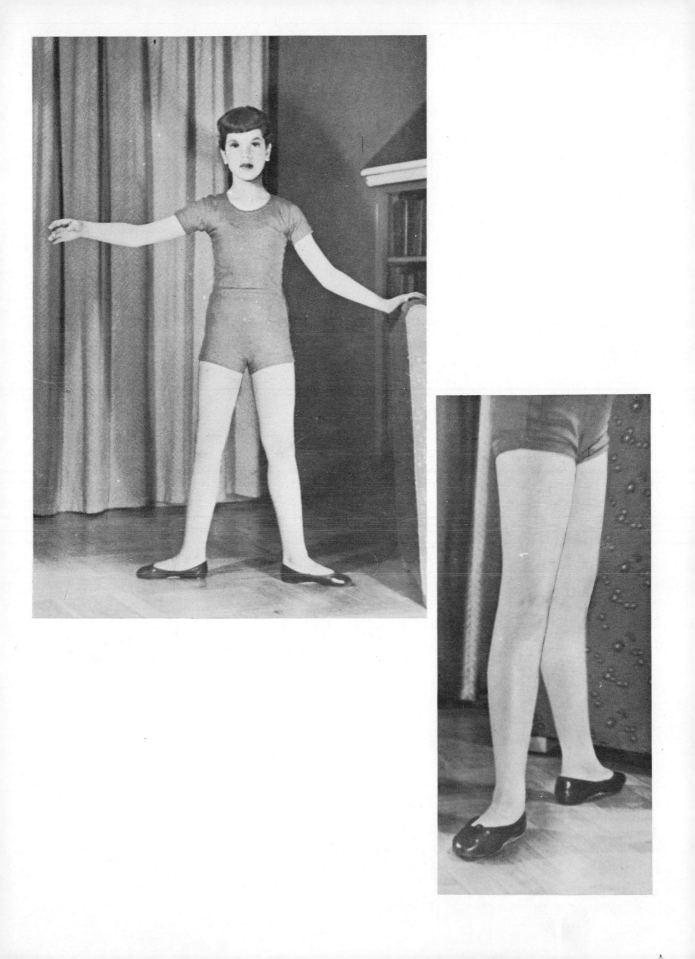

Third Position

From second position, pull your right foot in until it is alongside your left, with your right heel up against the arch of your left foot. Your legs and feet must remain well turned out.

Third position is a preparation for fifth position and is seldom used, but it is a necessary step in the series.

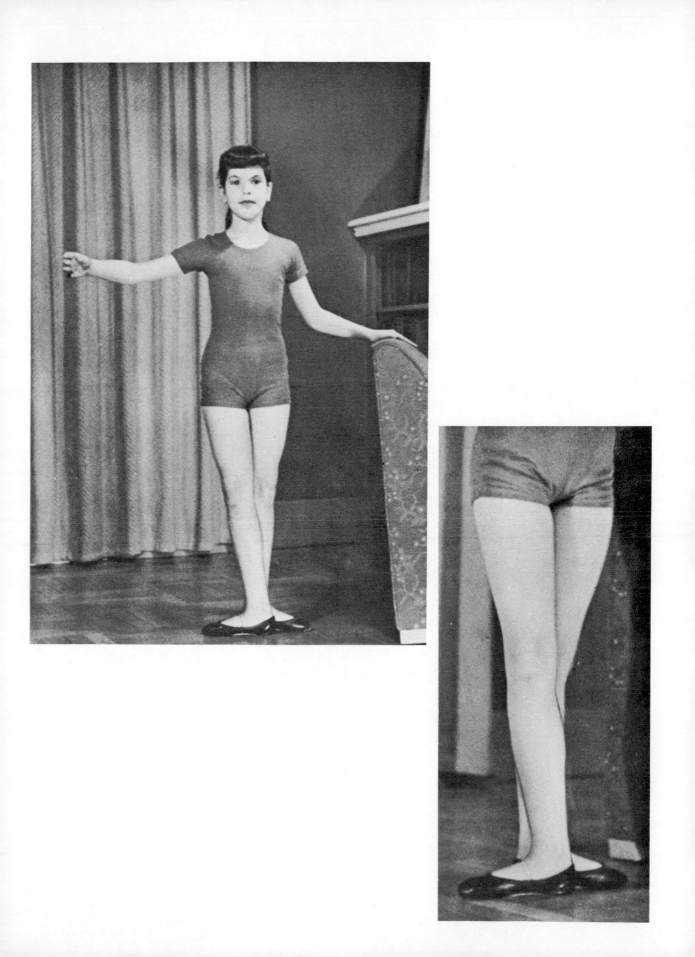

Fourth Position

From third position, slide your right foot forward for a distance equal to the length of your foot. Keep your legs and feet well turned out. The heel of your right foot should now be in line with the toes of your left foot. The weight of your body must be centered over your legs. Look at the close-up photograph of fourth position and you will see that the legs make an exact upside-down "V" with the body directly above.

You may find fourth position a little difficult to do at first, but as your turn-out develops it will become easier.

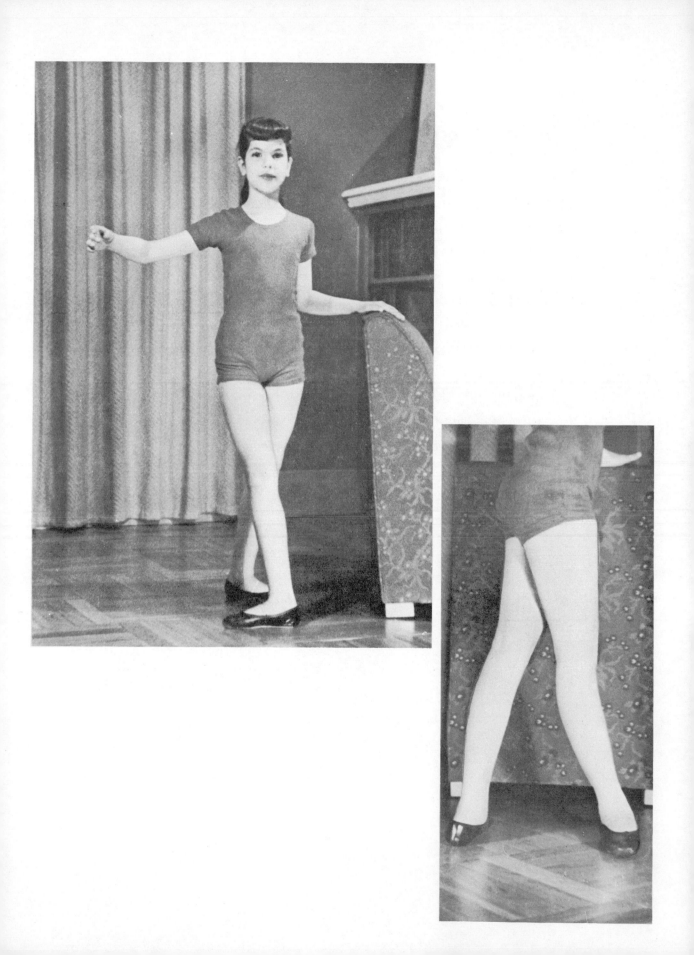

Fifth Position

From fourth position, slide your right foot straight backward, keeping it constantly turned out, until it is flat alongside your left foot. Now you will have to remember to keep your knees straight because your front knee will want very much to bend a little. Keep your back straight by pulling your seat muscles tightly under you and pushing your shoulders downward. Stomach must be in; chin up; right arm extended in a soft curve, palm forward.

You are now in fifth position, which is the most often used position in ballet dancing.

You have just done the five positions by moving your RIGHT leg. Now turn and face the other way, place your right hand on the *barre* and do the positions by moving your LEFT leg.

18

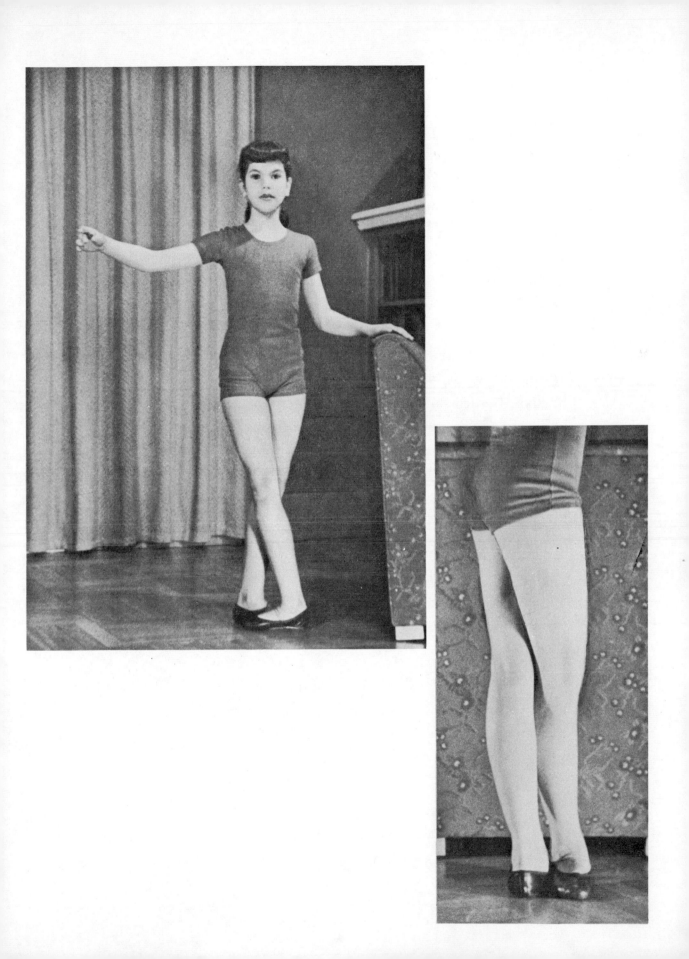

Demi-Plié

IN FIRST POSITION

In French, the word *plié* means "bend" and *demi* means "half"— so this ballet term says that the legs do a half bend. *Pliés* are very important in ballet. Almost every movement uses some types of *plié*. It is the exercise with which dancers start their practice, and ballerinas always do some *pliés* to warm up and prepare their muscles just before a performance.

Stand facing the *barre* in first position. Now bend the knees slowly, pushing outward from the hips, knees turned out, feet remaining flat on the floor. Return slowly to the straight position.

The lower picture shows how *demi-pliés* should be done. Your feet do not move at all and your body remains straight and centered over your legs. Your seat must be held in tightly and kept directly under you.

All *pliés* should be done with smooth, even motions—do not pop up and down like a jack-in-the-box.

It is only at the very beginning that you do *demi-pliés* facing the *barre*. Once you have gotten the feeling of the movements, do them alongside the *barre,* placing only one hand on it for balance.

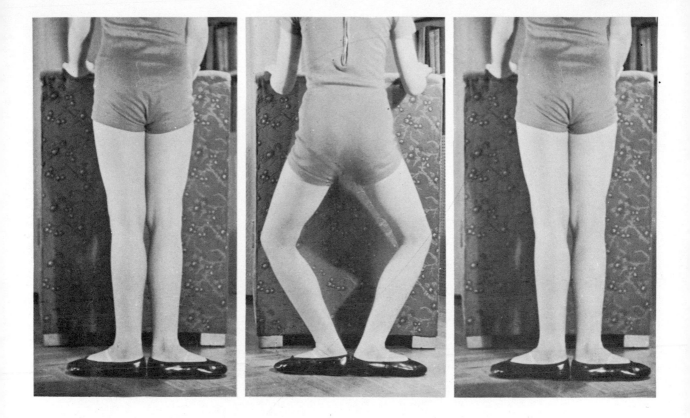

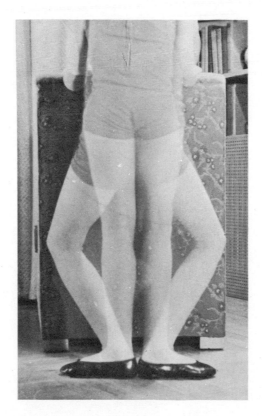

Demi-Plié (continued)

IN SECOND POSITION

From first position, slide your foot out to second position, having the weight of your body well centered over your legs. Now *demi-plié* as in the picture, keeping your knees turned out.

Do *demi-pliés* several times in each position . . . up . . . down . . . up . . . down, slowly, evenly, smoothly.

IN FOURTH POSITION

From second position, slide your foot back to third position and then immediately forward to fourth position. Here as you *demi-plié* you will have to be careful because your back knee will want very much to point forward toward the floor and inward toward your front leg. Keep it well pushed out, at the same time remembering to keep your feet flat so that your little toes do not rise from the floor. It will help if you remember to keep your weight centered over your legs.

IN FIFTH POSITION

From fourth position slide your foot backward to fifth position. Then, as you *demi-plié,* keep your feet firmly on the floor and your body straight.

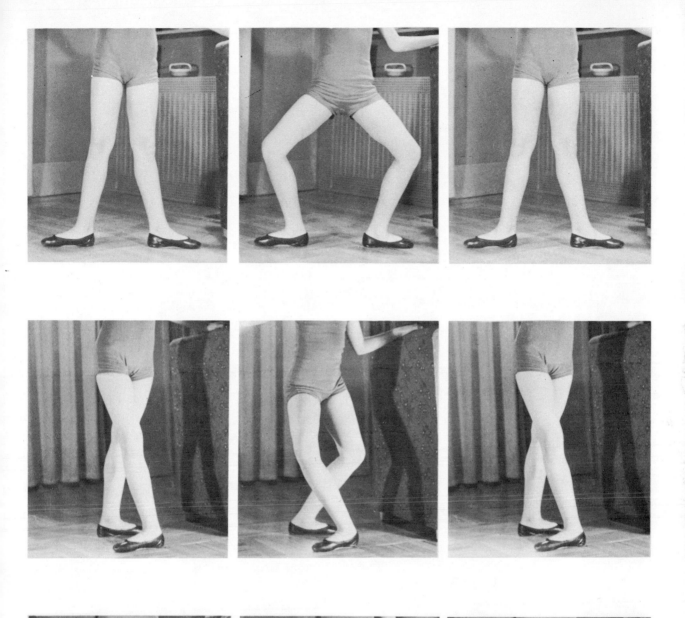

Grand Plié

IN FIRST POSITION

After practicing *demi-plié*, go on to *grand plié*, or "full bend."

Stand at the *barre* in first position. Slowly *plié*, but this time when you reach *demi-plié*, don't stop—keep on with the *plié* until you are as far down as you can go, knees well out, seat tucked under. Your heels rise only after you have passed *demi-plié*, and should come off the floor as little as possible. Return slowly to the straight position.

Grand pliés develop the turn-out; they strengthen the ankles; they make the body supple and strong. They stretch and strengthen the "Achilles' tendon" in your heel and this is so essential to good dancing.

Be patient and thorough with the *plié*. It is one of the first things you learn, and it is something you will never stop doing in your entire career as a dancer.

IN SECOND POSITION

Slide your foot to second position, keeping your weight well centered. Now *plié* as far as you can, keeping your knees firmly turned out. Your heels must not leave the floor. In *grand plié*, second position is the only position where your heels do not leave the floor.

As in all *pliés*, do several, one right after the other, always remembering to move slowly and deliberately up and down.

24

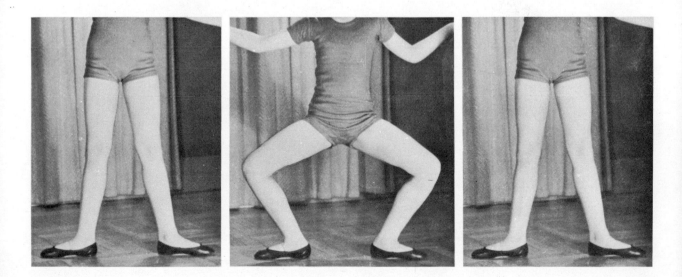

Grand Plié (continued)

IN FOURTH POSITION

Slide your foot to fourth position. Now, as you do *grand plié*, just as in *demi-plié*, you will have to watch your back knee which will try very hard to point downward and inward. Keep your weight centered over your legs.

IN FIFTH POSITION

From fourth position, slide your foot to fifth position. *Grand plié* as deep as you can without "sitting down" on your heels. You must always have control of your body—don't relax at the bottom of the *plié* and then pop upward. The movement must be steady and careful . . . down . . . up . . . down . . . up . . . and so on.

Watch your heels, too. When you are at the bottom of the *plié* they should feel as though you are trying to push them down toward the floor.

26

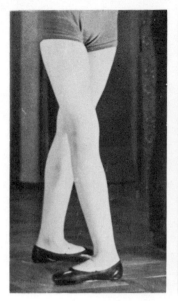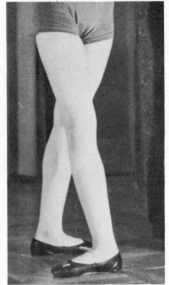

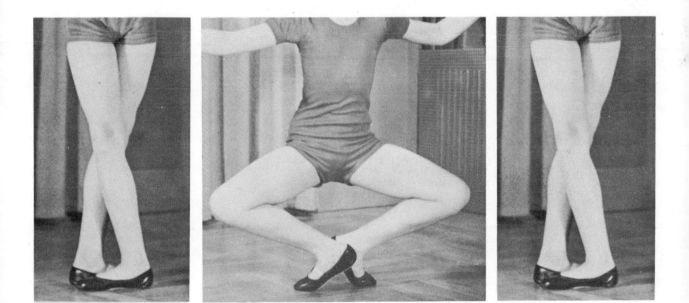

Battement Tendu

FRONT

Stand at the *barre* in fifth position, right foot front. Slide your right foot forward into a firm, well-arched point, as far as it can go without lifting your toe from the floor. Start the movement with the entire foot, the heel leaving the floor only after it is lifted by the stretch of your leg. All during the movement, the weight of your body is on the left leg, while your working leg moves freely back and forth . . . stretch forward . . . back to fifth . . . stretch forward . . . back to fifth . . . and so on.

Your leg must be so well turned out, with the heel turned far enough to the front, that your foot sets quite properly into place as your leg returns to fifth position.

SIDE

From fifth position, right foot front, slide your foot to the side in a firm point, then slide back to fifth, right foot behind. Your toe should not leave the floor and your knee should never bend. The only part of your body that moves is the working leg. Your hips must be tight and must not swing around as your leg slides. Don't lean away and pull at the *barre*—keep your body erect.

Return your foot to fifth-back and fifth-front, in turns.

BACK

Finish your side *tendu* with your foot in fifth position back. Now slide your foot straight back into a firm point, leg turned out and heel forward as far as possible. Slide back to fifth.

28

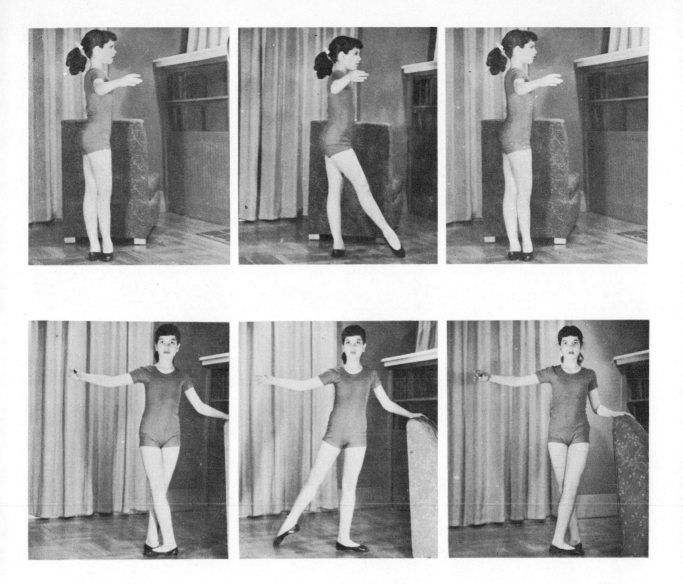

Battement Tendu with Plié

FRONT

This movement starts out the same as the simple *battement tendu* which you have just learned. But this time, *plié* while your leg is returning to fifth position. Your foot is tucked into place at the deepest point in the *plié*. As you stretch forward for the next *tendu,* you rise from your *plié* and are quite straight again as your toe reaches its farthest point.

SIDE

Battement tendu to the side and *plié* as you are returning your foot to fifth position. You do: *plié* . . . straighten up as your foot slides outward . . . *plié* as your foot slides back.

Return your foot to fifth-back and fifth-front, in turns.

BACK

Battement tendu to the back, and *plié* as you return to fifth.

30

Port de Bras with Body Bend

Now for the first time you will begin to move your arms independently of your body movement.

Stand at the *barre* in fifth position, right foot front, arm extended to the side. Keeping your shoulders firmly pushed down, start bending forward slowly, stomach muscles drawn tight. Stretch forward and downward as far as you can go, moving only from the hips. As you bend, your chin remains high and your head follows last, dropping forward at the end with your forehead trying to get as close to your knees as possible. Your arm follows your body downward, the wrist moving first and the fingers following softly until you lightly touch your foot.

Now start to rise, moving from the hips, back straight, stomach muscles pulled in, arm softly curved. Continue the movement until you are bending backward from the hips. Then, as you return slowly upright, your arm moves outward in a flowing motion to its position extended at the side.

Things to watch in body bending: Your shoulders must never hunch up—keep them pushed down so that your neck "feels long." In bending backward, your back remains straight and bends at the hips and not at the waist. In a young girl, the spine is supple and it is easier to arch the back at the waistline, but this is not correct.

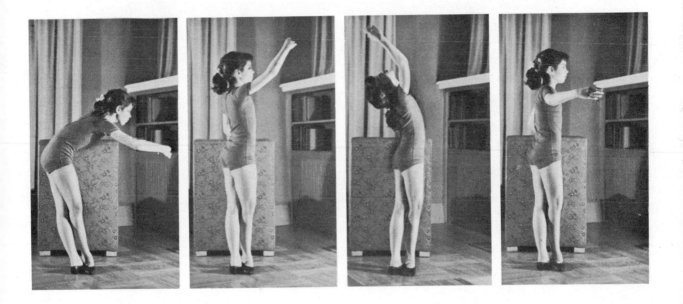

Ronds de Jambe à Terre

In this exercise, your foot draws a huge letter D on the floor.

Stand in first position. *Battement tendu* to the front. From the farthest forward point, swing your leg outward and around in a large half circle until your toe is pointed behind you as in the picture. Then bring your leg forward (keeping it always turned out) until it slides back into first position again.

Make the circles smoothly and evenly, one after another without stopping, four times starting forward and circling around to the back, and four times starting backward and circling around to the front.

And—just as a reminder again—don't forget to repeat everything with the other leg!

Watch these points carefully:

Your body must remain quite steady on your supporting leg—nothing moves but your working leg. Your hips must not swing around in circles following your leg.

The knee of your working leg must never bend. Keep this in mind particularly as your leg comes through first position.

Keep your foot firmly pointed at the forward, side and back positions.

Your toe never leaves the floor, and your heel leaves it only when it can no longer reach the floor.

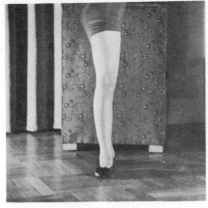

First position . . .

. . . foot slides forward . . .

. . to *battement tendu* front .

. . . and outward . . .

. . to *battement tendu* side . .

. . and continues the slide . .

. . to *battement tendu* back . . then forward in a straight line . . . to first position.

Frappé

FRONT

Stand beside the *barre* in fifth position. Raise your right foot to your ankle, keeping your knee well turned out. Now thrust your right foot forward sharply—letting it just brush the floor as it goes—until your leg is straight and your toe just a few inches off the floor. Then return the foot to its position on the left ankle.

Since *frappé* in French means "beat" or "strike," these movements must be done briskly with a sort of beating action. At all times your hips and supporting leg must be tight and unmoving.

SIDE

As you finish *frappé* to the front, do a series of the same movement to the side. Be sure that your leg goes directly to the side, and not half-front or half-back. For the side exercise, you bring your foot to the ankle first in back, then in front, in turns. It goes: Thrust out . . . return to back . . . thrust out . . . return to front, and so on. And don't forget to brush smartly as your leg goes out.

BACK

Finish side *frappé* with your leg on the back of your ankle, and you are ready to start *frappé* to the back. The action is the same, your leg moving sharply straight back.

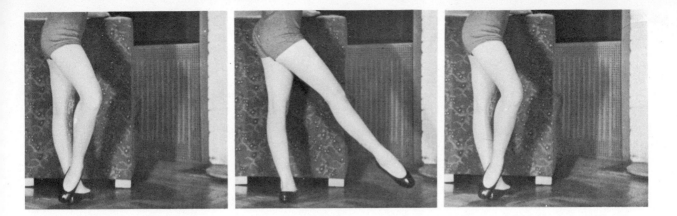

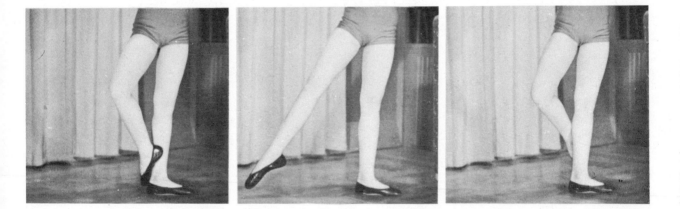

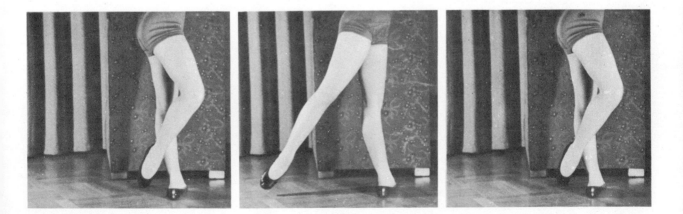

Petit Battement

Stand at the *barre* in fifth position. Lift your right foot (keeping your knee well turned out) until it is touching the front of your ankle. Now move your foot quickly around to touch the back of your ankle. The moving foot, always well pointed, travels closely around the supporting leg, which remains straight. All the movement comes from the knee, which acts like a hinge with the leg moving back and forth below it. The pictures show this movement as seen from front and side.

This exercise must be done briskly—back, front, back, front, and so on.

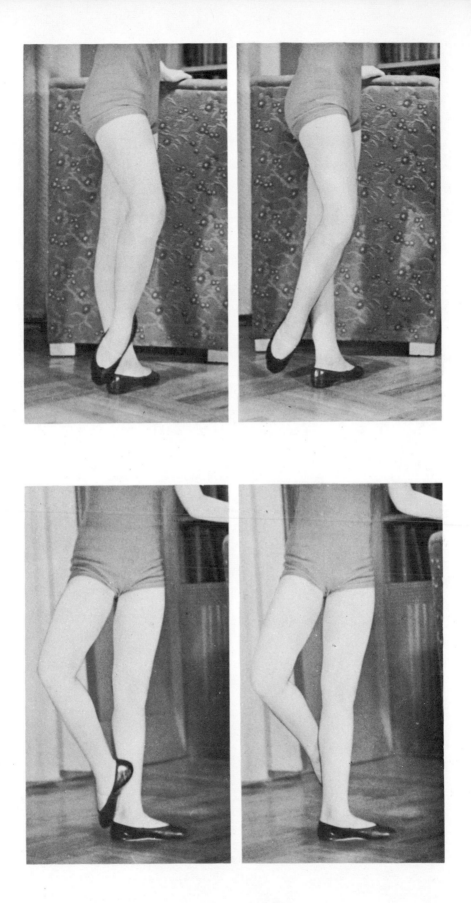

Passé

Stand at the *barre* in fifth position, right foot front. Raise your right leg as shown in the picture, knee well turned out, foot firmly arched. Your right toe should touch your left leg at a point just a little toward the front of the leg.

Now lower your right leg to fifth position, back.

Repeat *passé* several times: Front . . . up . . . back . . . up . . . front; and so on.

Make the movements smoothly and firmly, being sure not to jerk your body and to keep your supporting leg quite straight while your working leg is moving.

40

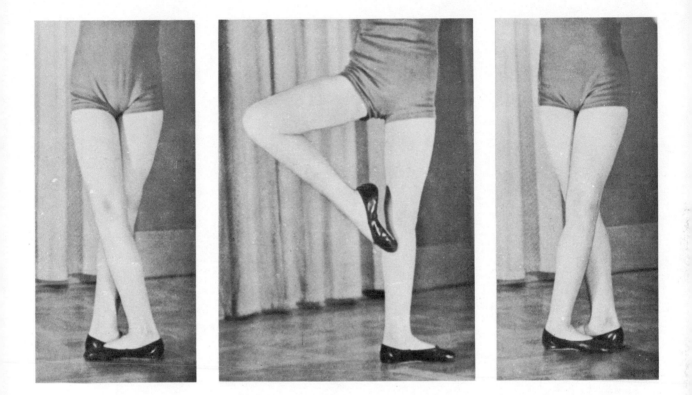

Grand Battement

FRONT

Stand at the *barre* in fifth position, right foot front. Keeping your leg turned out and your heel forward, raise your leg to a level position straight front. Lower your leg again to fifth position.

The important thing in *grand battement* is to do the movement properly rather than to try for great height. Don't throw your leg as high as you can and then let it fall back; raise it firmly, keep it straight and lower it with full control. Your supporting leg must be straight and your body must not be jerked with the effort of your upward swing.

SIDE

Raise your leg sidewise to a level position and return it to fifth position front and fifth position back, in turns. Don't pull away from the *barre* when doing *grand battement* to the side; keep your body erect.

BACK

Finish side *grand battement* with right foot in back. Then raise your leg backward, but only as far as you can without bending the knee. Lower again to fifth-back.

Practice *grand battement* with steady, smooth movements, thinking of it as a "lifting" movement rather than a "kicking" movement.

Relevé

Face the *barre* in second position. Rise on half-toe, legs straight. Lower again.

In ballet dancing, "half-toe" means standing on the balls of your feet, with your heels pulled up hard. You must not rise to the tips of your toes.

Tighten your ankles when you are on half-toe so that your feet don't wiggle back and forth. Your legs must be well turned out so that your heels are as far front as possible.

Do this exercise briskly . . . up, down, up, down, up, down . . . eight times. Then *relevé* once more and stay on half-toe, keeping all your muscles firm until you feel you have your balance. Next raise your arms to the side to shoulder level. Keep this pose for a moment, then lower gently to first position.

You must learn to keep your balance without any help or support. This is not possible unless you make your muscles work hard. Keep your back muscles tight, your hips firm, your seat muscles tucked under, your stomach pulled in, and your shoulders pushed down.

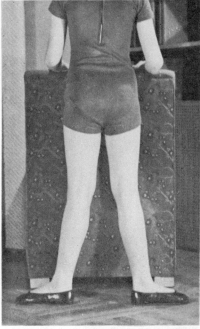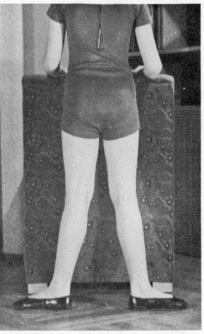

Second position . . .   . . . rise on half-toe . . .   . . . down again to second.

Balance.

Arabesque

The *arabesque* is one of the basic poses in classical ballet. There are various kinds of *arabesques,* and you can begin your study of them with the help of the *barre.*

Face the *barre* in fifth position, right foot back, both hands resting on the *barre. Battement tendu* to the back, then raise your leg from the floor, as in the photograph. Now take your right hand off the *barre.* Then, as soon as you feel that all your muscles are tight and you have your balance, lift your left hand from the *barre* also. You should be able to keep this position for a moment without swaying; then return your hands to the *barre* and lower your leg to fifth position.

Be sure that both legs—your supporting leg as well as your raised leg —are absolutely straight, with never the slightest bend in your knees at any point in the movement. All leg movements are done from the hip, with your hip and seat muscles tight. The toes of your raised foot must be firmly pointed, the foot turned out so well that the heel cannot be seen from the side. Remember to keep your shoulders pushed down hard— they may try to hunch up as you raise your leg.

Fifth position . . .

. . . *battement tendu* back . . .

. . . raise leg . . .

. . . one arm up . . .

. . . balance.

Port de Bras

By now you have become familiar enough with some of the exercises so that you can leave the *barre* for part of your practice and do some center work.

Stand in fifth position with your arms curving down in front of your body, fingers almost touching, as in the first picture. Keep your arms curved this way as you raise them in front of you to waist height and then continue upward until they are overhead, just a little forward of straight up. Now open your arms to the sides. As they pass shoulder level, turn your palms downward, continuing to lower your arms until they are again in starting position.

From beginning to end of this *port de bras* there is no pause. It is a continuous smoothly flowing movement, as if your arms were trailing through water. Don't wave your hands in the air like the flip-flop of a paint brush, and don't curve your fingers like claws. And, as always, remember to keep your shoulders well pushed down and your neck "tall."

When your arms are overhead, they should make an oval-shaped frame, a little forward of your head. You must not push your arms straight up overhead or your shoulders will have to hunch up and your movements will not be free.

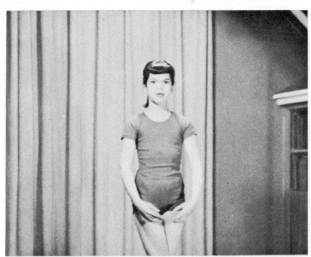

Arms curved low . . .

. . . raise to waist height . . .

. . . then upward . . .

. . . and open outward, palms up . . .

. . . turning them gently downward . . .

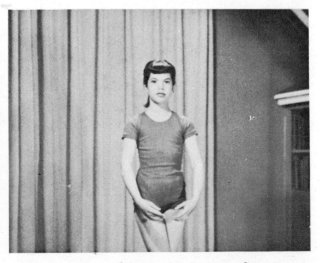

. . . as you bring your arms down.

Glissade

In ballet, in order to move from one place to another, special dance steps are used instead of ordinary walking steps. *Glissade* is such a movement.

Stand in fifth position, left foot front, arms curved low. Slide your left foot to the side, firmly pointed, and at the same time raise your arms to the side. Now shift your weight to your left foot while sliding your right foot behind it into fifth position *plié*. Your hands come down again as you finish the *glissade*.

You can do a series of *glissades,* one after another, and they become smooth waves of motion across the floor.

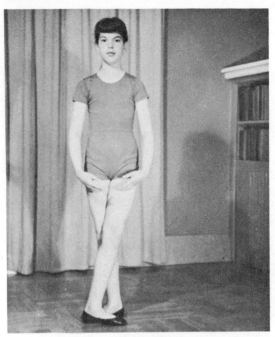

Fifth position . . .

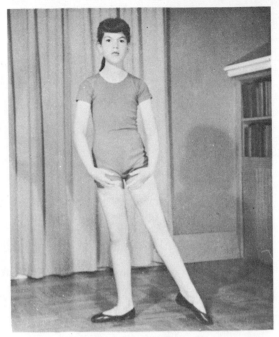

. . . left foot steps out . . .

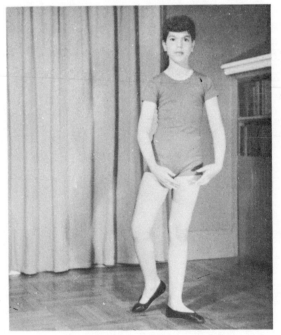

. . . right foot glides behind . . .

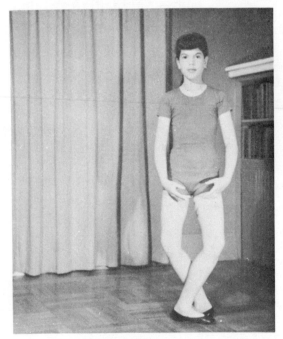

. . . into fifth *plié* again.

Changement de Pieds

This is a jump in which you exchange the positions of your feet while you are in the air.

Stand in fifth position, arms curved low, right foot in front. *Demi-plié*, then jump straight up and interchange your foot positions while you are in the air, landing with your left foot in front. Your legs must remain tightly together with toes well pointed while you are rising. It is only after you start down that you change your feet quickly so that they are again in fifth position, but with LEFT foot front as they touch the floor.

Don't fling your arms around in the air as you jump; keep them as well as you can in the starting position. Don't arch your back — keep your body straight all the while.

These jumps should be made one after another, smoothly and evenly like a bouncing ball, each time changing foot positions, back-to-front, front-to-back. It is not just a matter of crossing your legs and crashing down on the floor. You should come down lightly in a good fifth position *demi-plié*, rising smoothly again into the next *changement de pieds*.

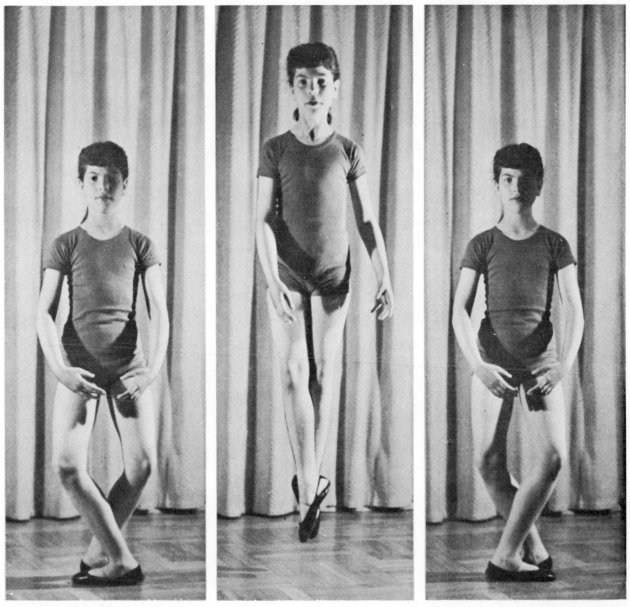

Start with right foot front . . .   . . . up . . .   . . . finish with left foot front.

Pas de Chat

This step is a lot of fun. In French, *pas de chat* means "cat-step" and that's just what it looks like.

Stand in fifth position, left foot front. *Plié* as you bring your left foot up to your right knee and jump sidewise in the air, landing on your left foot. Your right foot follows quickly after, coming down behind your left knee, as in the picture, to fifth position *plié,* foot front. You might imagine that you are leaping sidewise over a log, pulling each leg high in order to clear. Do several *pas de chats,* one right after another.

Things to remember are to keep your knees always well turned out and your body straight as you jump. When you practice this step, think of a cat—how lightly it pounces, paws lifting high, landing gracefully and noiselessly.

Starting with left foot front . . .

. . . raise left foot high to leap . . .

. . . and land on left foot,
right foot following down . . .

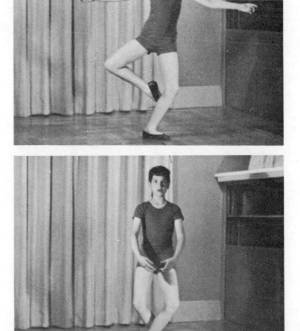

. . . into fifth position *plié*.

Pas de Bourrée

Like *glissade,* this movement is very useful in a dance for getting from one spot to another.

Stand in fifth position, left foot front. *Plié,* at the same time raising your right foot behind your left leg as in the first picture. Now lower your right leg behind your left, shift your weight to your right leg as you step aside with your left leg into second position, half-toe. Then cross your right leg in front of your left and as you put your weight onto your right leg, *plié* and lift your left leg, behind your right, as shown in the last picture. You can start right back again from this point, doing a series of *bourrées* to the right and to the left. Your arms follow the direction of your movements, as in the photographs.

This may sound confusing, but it will become clear if, at first, you study the pictures carefully and then have someone read the instructions aloud as you go through the steps.

In *pas de bourrée,* be sure that your knees are always well turned outward, and that your foot is firmly pointed as you raise it behind the other leg. While on half-toe in second position, your knees must be quite straight and feet strongly arched.

Right foot up . . .

. . . put it down in back . . .

. . . left foot out to second . . .

. . . right foot goes in front . . .

. . . left foot up.

Révérence

At the end of the lesson or performance, you bow graciously in acknowledgment to your teacher or your audience.

Here is a simple *révérence*. *Plié* with your back leg, pointing with your front leg, arms out to the side.

Things to Remember

POSTURE

A dancer must always be sure to stand and walk properly. In the first picture, notice the humped shoulders, sagging stomach, curved backbone. In the second picture you can see that proper posture is much more attractive and it is much better for your health, too. Tighten your stomach muscles. Push your shoulders down. Keep your chin and head up. Pull your seat muscles under tightly and you will see how this straightens your back.

THE ARM

For most *barre* work, the arm is extended to the side in a gentle curve slightly below shoulder level. Keep the hand soft and graceful, palm turned forward. The elbow must be turned upward and kept at the back of the arm—this means that anyone standing directly in front of you should never be able to see the point of your elbow showing below your arm.

THE HAND

The hand must extend from the arm in a soft line. The thumb should be turned slightly inward under the palm. The fingers should be held quite closely together and not spread in all directions.

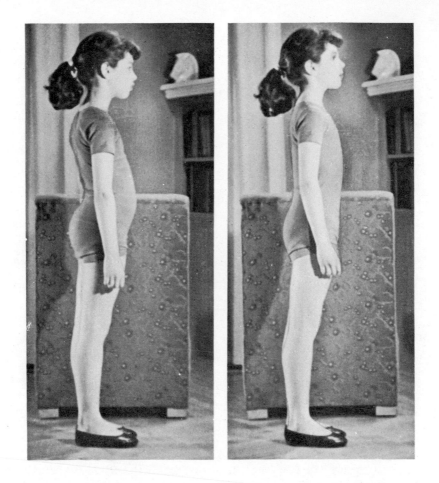

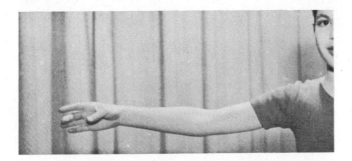

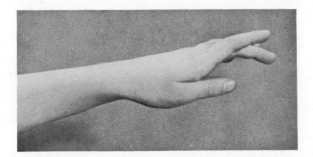

Things to Remember (continued)

THE FOOT

This is a well-pointed foot. In the left photograph you may see what is happening inside the ballet shoe. The toes are pointed and the muscle at the back of the heel is pulling up hard, making the foot well arched.

SICKLING

This means pointing the foot incorrectly by arching its outer side instead of the inner side. Whether the pointed foot is in the air or on the ground, it must not curve as shown in the left picture, where the foot takes on the shape of the grass sickle used on farms. The other picture shows the correct way. Watch for sickling particularly in *battement tendu* and *passé*.

ROLLING ARCHES

In all these exercises, your smaller toes must do their share of carrying the weight of your body. Make them do this by trying always to press them down on the floor. This will help to prevent your arches from flattening inward and keep your weight off the joint of your big toe, which otherwise might enlarge and make toe work very difficult for you later.

PLIES

The left picture shows some of the mistakes made most often in *pliés* —arches are rolled, knees point forward, seat sticks out, stomach sags, head droops. The other picture shows a more accurate *plié*—shoulders pushed down; seat muscles drawn tight so that the seat is almost over the heels; knees are turned out, helping to keep the arches from rolling. So many things to remember at once! But good ballet dancing requires good *pliés*.

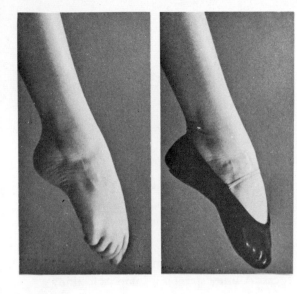

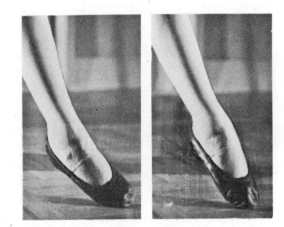

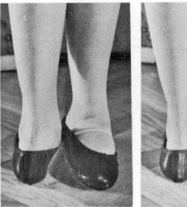

French Terms Used in Ballet

arabesque (ar-a-BESK). One of the basic poses in classical ballet. The body is poised on one leg with the other extended behind without bending the knee. Based on this, there are many kinds of arabesques, always having the effect of a long, well formed, balanced line from finger-tips to toe-tips.

barre (bar). A hand rail along the wall of the dance studio, used to help keep the balance during practice and limbering-up exercises.

battement tendu (baht-MAW tawn-DU). *Battement*: beats, kicks. *Tendu*: stretched, reached. A movement where the foot slides outward, without leaving the floor, until the straight leg is extended as far as it can go, pointed toe touching the floor.

changement de pieds (shanzh-maw d' pyay). *Changement*: changing, shifting. *Pieds*: feet. A jump straight up from fifth position, reversing the position of the feet while in the air and landing again in fifth.

demi-plié (d'mee plee-AY). *Demi*: half. *Plié*: bend, fold. A bending of the knees, legs turned out, heels remaining on the floor.

frappé (frah-PAY). Strike, knock. A small, sharp kick, with the foot starting from and returning to the ankle of the supporting leg.

glissade (glee-SAHD). Slide. A smooth, step-sliding movement, a gliding step.

grand battement (grahn baht-MAW). *Grand*: large. *Battement*: beats, kicks. A high kicking movement of the leg without bending the knee.

grand plié (grahn plee-AY). *Grand*: large. *Plié*: bend, fold. A very deep bending of the knees, legs turned out.

pas de bourrée (pah d' boor-AY). *Pas*: step. *Bourrée*: weaving. A stepping movement in which the legs seem to weave in and out.

pas de chat (pah d' SHAH). *Pas*: step. *Chat*: cat. A lithe, springing jump, something like the delicate pouncing of a cat.

passé (pahss-AY). Passed. A bent position of the leg, with the foot at the knee of the supporting leg, while passing the leg from one position to another.

plié (plee-AY). Bend. A bending of the knees, either halfway or full.

petit battement (p'tee baht-MAW). *Petit*: Small, tiny. *Battement*: beats, kicks. Small beats of the foot around the ankle of the supporting leg.

port de bras (por d' brah). *Port*: carry. *Bras*: arms. Any carrying, or movement, of the arms.

relevé (re-lev-AY). Raise. To rise up on the toes.

révérence (ray-vay-RAWNSS). A gesture of respect, a bow. Any one of many kinds of curtsies or bows.

ronds de jambe à terre (rawn d' zhahmb a tair). *Ronds*: circles. *Jambe*: leg. *à terre*: on the ground. Large half circles traced on the floor by the foot.

sur les pointes (soor lay pwant). *Sur*: on. *Pointes*: points, or tips. Standing on the tips of the toes.